On the Hill

On the Hill

Bessie Marlin Mason

*Love to Edna
from
Aunt Bessie*

Vagrom Chap Book No. 17, Sparrow Press
a Purdue Poets Cooperative Book distributed by Sparrow

ISBN: 0-935552-01-4
A Purdue Poets Cooperative Book
Copyright (c) 1980 by Felix and Selma Stefanile

Sparrow Press
103 Waldron Street
West Lafayette, Indiana 47906

- 7 The Hill
- 9 Weather Report
- 10 Return to Summer Quarters
- 11 Come
- 12 Real Estate
- 14 Morning in April
- 15 New Fence
- 16 The Avicide
- 18 Song of Rights
- 20 New Spring House
- 21 Conflict
- 22 The Buzzard
- 24 Turtle Pace
- 25 The Fall of a Walnut Tree
- 26 Unwanted
- 27 Headlines
- 28 Garden on the Bend
- 30 Calf Astray
- 32 The Return
- 33 Visitation
- 34 This is My House
- 35 Big Black Dog
- 36 Angus in a Hereford Pasture
- 37 Little Old Lady in a Big Old House
- 38 Inflection
- 39 Twilight Call
- 40 Pennies
- 42 Spring Song in January

On the Hill

This book is for Olive and for all of my friends who love the country.

THE HILL

This hill is alma mater of
All creatures here, awake or sleeping;
She holds the rhythm of their lives
Fondly in her mystic keeping.

WEATHER REPORT

March came in like a soft lamb bleating,
Tremolo voice young and unsteady;
March came in like a new colt waiting
With legs for walking but not quite ready;
March came in like a kitten purring
Under the comfort of warm winds stroking.
March went out like a lion roaring,
Pleased with the noise of his own provoking;
March went out like a tiger pawing,
Tearing the air with sleet claws scratching;
March went out like a wild mare neighing,
White mane flying, long neck stretching.

So March, the capricious, again has cavorted
Into the past with his frivolous weather,
Variform pieces unmated, unsorted,
Lion and lamb and all together.

RETURN TO SUMMER QUARTERS

The latch is lifted; the wide gate swings;
    The pasture grass is green and cool.
High in the cedar the mockingbird sings;
    Frog voices pour from the willow-rimmed pool.

Around the bend a white door gleams;
    The quick lock yields to the click of my key.
The little house, wrapped in its winter dreams,
    Wakes to welcome the summer and me.

COME

All is ready.
>   Enter: spring,
Done with coy
>   Loitering,

Calls "Come back"
>   And birds fly home;
Calls "Come out"
>   And leaf buds come.

Calls "Come down"
>   And raindrops fall;
Calls "Come up"
>   And grass grows tall.

Life begins
>   To glow and hum
When the spring
>   Is calling "Come."

REAL ESTATE

"This hill is mine," I said, "this hill
And everything on it, all my own,
The high, quick cry of the whip-poor-will,
The shadow slanting across the stone..."
    The red fox had nothing to say to me then,
    He was hiding sullenly in his den;
    At midnight, though, and a long time after
    He barked at me with scornful laughter.

"Even this little brook is mine,"
My possessive fingers wrote in the sand,
And I lolled in the shade of a wild grapevine
And ruffled the stream with caressing hand.
    But the waters were racing away from me,
    Singing, "The brook belongs to the sea
    And the brook is off on its ocean trip:
    What prattle is this about ownership?"

I tried to tear loose a round gray rock
From the grip of the earth, but the earth held tight
With effortless power that seemed to mock
The futile force of my struggling might.
    "Mine," said the earth, and the earth held on,
    "Mine long after you are gone."
    A chipmunk whisked by with a questioning glance,
    "Who is this new insignificance?"

"What is mine, then?" I asked the sun.
"This day," said the sun, and the day before,
To-morrow likely another one;
By the grace of Heaven there may be more."
    The red fox chuckled, I think, "And so,
    My fellow-transient, now you know,"
    For he barked that night and all nights after
    With friendly tones in his midnight laughter.

MORNING IN APRIL

This hour is bright with the glow of dawn
    And the joy the jaunty cardinal sings;
It is sweet with the breath of the apple bloom
    And alive with growing things.

There are dark, dark hours that have gone before,
    There are dull, gray hours that are yet to be,
But this is a radiant, lovely one
    And it races away from me.

O Time, with your long array of hours,
    Please stop for a little space;
Let me take this one out and hold it awhile,
    I will put it back in its place.

NEW FENCE

Today these roving young twin shorthorns learned
That strong, well-woven lines of shining wire
Are barriers. Conceding defeat, they turned
Their faces, wistful with the mute desire
For neighbor's grass, back to their late-scorned own
And browsed content beside the fence between
What they'd no right to and what was well-known
As theirs and found it good again and green.
    I wonder if they learned that resignation
    Is better sauce for pasture than frustration.

THE AVICIDE

In the garden today a crime occured:
A cat sneaked in and murdered a bird
                         And later
                         Ate her.

The bird flew high; the cat crouched low,
On his face a green-eyed glow
                         Beaming
                         And gleaming.

The bird flew low; the cat leaped high,
Avid purpose in his eye
                         Vicious
                         Pernicious.

One nimble spring! like hideous dream
His sharp teeth closed on her frightened scream.
                         Ferocious!
                         Atrocious!

He crunched her bones, he lapped her blood,
He chewed her flesh and it was good.
                         The savage!
                         What ravage!

He smacked his lips and wiped his claws
And licked his murderous little paws
                         Nicely,
                         Precisely.

He lay down smug and satisfied
With never a qualm for the bird inside,
      His dinner,
      The sinner.

O come, Avenger, and begin
Destroying those nine lives of him;
      Dismay him
      And slay him

And dig him a grave that the vile worms love
And place this epitaph above
      To abase him,
      Disgrace him:

"Here lies a cat that lived and purred
And murdered a poor little innocent bird
      And munched her
      And crunched her.

He lived a year and a day beside
And died long after he ought to have died."
      Earth, flay him,
      Decay him;
      Hold him,
      Enfold him;
      Scorn him
      And mourn him;
      Regret him,
      Forget him.

SONG OF RIGHTS

At twilight I walked, or near twilight,
On a woodsy hill. I had a right,
For the hill and the wood and the path are mine
Morning or evening or any time
Of any day or any night.

I stopped to uproot a defacing weed,
Not wishing my hill to be host to its seed,
All unaware that a yellow race
Of wasps was living at its base.
Vespids attack with incredible speed.

Six tiny arrows astonished my flesh
And stung me homeward like wind-driven trash.
Well, wasps have a right to defend their home
Against whatever marauders may come
With any fair weapon that they wish.

Every home-loving creature should.
You would and I would — everyone would.
And I have a right to walk my hill
And banish unsightly weeds at will;
This isn't a question of bad or good.

It isn't a question of right or wrong
And who are intruders and who belong.
It is only a case of two rights that collided,
And which right is more right will remain undecided
Long after the songs of this singer are sung.

Tomorrow I'll walk my hill as secure
In my right to walk as I was before
The yellow jackets made such a stir,
But wiser, of course, and warier
And more circumspect – or a little more.

NEW SPRING HOUSE

We have captured a wild thing running free,
Routed our quarry with shovel and pick,
Closed in upon it relentlessly
Stone by stone and brick by brick;
We have made it conform to a changing age:
We have put the pasture spring in a cage.

CONFLICT

Nature wants this hillside back in jungle.
Man is determined not to have it so:
His scythe and shears are sharp for vine and tangle,
His hours are tuned to tools that snip and mow.
This he has made a trim and pleasant acre,
Though now, of course, there's not much bird song here,
No haunts to tempt the woodland thrush and pecker;
The whip-poor-will has found a new frontier.
Nature seems just now accordant, really:
This well-groomed grass grows green, the breezes still
Play in the rich magnolia just as freely
As in the scrub oaks of the neighbor hill.
But let Man once go off and rest a little
Overtime, his sickles flung aside,
She soon will show him by what brief and brittle
Thread of time his sovereignty is tied.
She will move in with bramble, bush and tangle,
For Nature wants this hillside back in jungle.

THE BUZZARD

Rabbit, turtle, squirrel, and I
Watch that buzzard skim the sky.
Near motionless, his wide black wings
With no seeming flutterings
Bear him outward, upward, higher,
Propelled, perhaps, by strong desire
To scan the land with keen precision
And bring within the baleful vision
Of his speculative eye
What is dead or soon to die.
If his dark shadow swoops too near,
My woodland friends are stilled with fear,
And I am sad to think that they
Will be inevitable prey
Of carrion glutton such as he,
Their last speck of identity
Doomed to be one nauseous reek
Of breath upon his filthy beak.

But this vile fowl need not dispense
Toward me anticipative glance;
I claim Man's long prerogative
That all the generations give:
The sacred right to be interred
Too deep for clutches of such bird.

Of course, should homo sapiens
Rescind the culture of his gens
Becoming homo stupidus,
Unleash some savage, evil force
And fail to fetter it again,
The earth might not receive me then.
Instead of consecrated dust
My lot would be what all beasts' must:
With rabbit, turtle, squirrel I
Would lie beneath unsheltering sky,
Putrid mass on sun-scorched stones,
Talons laying bare my bones.

TURTLE PACE

By all the standards that I know
The pace of a turtle is very slow,
But it's likely, of course, that a sense of speed
Is something a turtle doesn't need.
He seems to remember what I had forgot
That a turtle's lot is a turtle's lot
And a turtle does what a turtle does
According to ancient turtle laws.
If there's something he hasn't, he does without it,
And there's nothing I need to say about it.

THE FALL OF A WALNUT TREE

Mr. Rickerson felled a tree.
    He did not want to fell it;
He loved the tree, so he told me,
    So that is the way I tell it.

A good old tree, he mused, betrayed,
    It gave nuts for the squirrels to gather
And cool green shade where his children played
    On the grass in the summer weather.

But a man who had come to the Rickerson door,
    Persuasive and demanding,
Said the tree was worth more, and that was for sure,
    Sawed down and sawed up than standing.

Mr. Rickerson felled it with a sigh,
    He did not want to fell it,
But he couldn't deny, and neither could I,
    That it made good sense to sell it.

It hurts to cut down a good tree, he said,
    With a hurt that is sharp like anger,
But his babes must be fed, he must look to their bread;
    Only money buys freedom from hunger.

And he fell to the limbs with a guilt-ridden ax,
    And, sparing hardly a splinter,
He stored them in stacks of neat little packs –
    It might be a long, hard winter.

So Mr. Rickerson felled a tree.
    "What has to be done, then so be it."
That is the way he saw it to-day,
    So that is the way I see it.

UNWANTED

She gave him birth. (She rues, I think, the day.)
    That bovine duty over, now she gives him
Nothing more except disdain. She moves away
    With quick, determined steps and leaves him.

He tries to follow, hunger in his eyes;
    She does not pause. She makes the distance wider
Between her and his plaintive, infant cries.
    She scorns to walk with a callow calf beside her.

At last he curls his weary self among
    Dry leaves to rest, unfed, unloved, neglected.
Poor little one! his mother taught him young
    The cruel, lonesome meaning of *rejected*.

HEADLINES

Any news on the hill to-day?
There is always news on a woodsy hill:
A turtle came by; he did not stay;
He hoisted his shell and ambled away.
The mockingbird sang and the whip-poor-will.

Two little foxes came up and played
With the Hereford calves, a daring thing,
But they haven't yet learned to be afraid.
A red calf was born in the sycamore shade.
Blackberries are ripe beyond the spring.

Lightning split a wild cherry tree;
A rainbow appeared with its seven soft hues;
Young rabbits hid in the timothy –
Oh, the hill is a newsy place to be
For anyone having a nose for news.

GARDEN ON THE BEND

On the seventh bend of Salt Creek lies
Agatha Siscoe's paradise,

A garden spot where summer has stored
Treasures of beauty, a priceless hoard.

Here, genius loci in calico,
Agatha hovers with sprinkler and hoe,

Her gray head bending in swift concern
Over parching petal or withering fern

Or lifted to gaze in silent delight
At a tanager poising his wings for flight.

Morning and evening and noontime too
She counts her riches as misers do:

Pansies and poppies and flaming phlox,
Roses and ruffled hollyhocks;

Bluejays splashing the sparkling pool,
Vivid and saucy and masterful;

An oriole on a grassy nest,
Butterflies flitting and pausing to rest.

Grace of tendril and grace of wings.
Color that dances and color that sings —

Such are the treasures her garden gives
On the seventh bend where Agatha lives.

Agatha, counting, adds one more:
The hard brown path from her neighbor's door.

And when Agatha Siscoe prays,
She merely gives thanks for summer days;

She asks no favors, seeks no bliss,
Desires no heaven better than this.

CALF ASTRAY

    He did not know, of course, how could he know
What years of wisdom teach (he had not had
A year's one half) that freedom like fenced pastures
Has its restrictions also. He had fed
On mother's milk when he had nuzzled at
That safe, warm source; had cropped the tender grass
That rose sun-bidden from the lavish earth.
The never-failing spring had slaked his thirst;
And for companionship were cousin calves
With whom he raced and gamboled on the hill
And bullfrogs splashing in the pasture pool
And birds to sing above him as he lay
At rest beneath a cedar, beech, or oak.
The hillside where he lived was wide and green
And there he roamed at will throughout the long
Sun-drenched or rain-cooled happy summer days.

    But he chafed at the restraining fence which kept
Him from the highway and curtailed his freedom:
He had a right to freedom to explore!
One day he broke a weak spot in the wire
And wriggled his whole Hereford body through
To freedom! But the grass along the road,
Seasoned with fumes of whizzing cars,
Was not so good as pasture grass. The slab
Of pavement did not please his fledgling hoofs,
And traffic noise bewildered his young ears.
Moreover, no one seemed to want him there.
Brakes shrieked and voices shrilled. In fright he found
That the fence that shut him in now shut him out.
And where was water? where companion calves?
And where the exit he himself had made?
He uttered a lonely, lost, deep-throated cry.

    Then quietly a human hand swung wide
The good white pasture gate. He darted through,
And all his seven fellow-kine came up
To welcome him with questions in their eyes:
Where did you go and why? And did you find
Freedom outside our fence? What was it like?

    Some new-found wisdom prompted his reply
As he gazed upon his native pasture fondly,
"Freedom, dear cousins, is here with a fence around it."

THE RETURN

Old Knobby was the hill that caused his fretting:
    He chafted at her; she shut the sky away,
Hid the westering sun before its setting,
    Stole an hour of sunshine from his day.

One day he climbed her summit, looking sunward
    To see the world beyond him and went down.
Old Knobby was the power that drove him onward
    To make his fortune in a hill-free town.

But hill dreams year by year awoke his sleeping;
    Sly Knobby lured him homeward track by track;
Now she holds him firmly in her keeping
    And proudly wears his mansion on her back.

VISITATION

The rapping spirits visit Mrs. Wevvle
    Any time of any night or day.
Are they welcome? Are they welcome, Mrs. Wevvle?
    Or do you wish that they would go away?

Sometimes they come to her at early milking,
    Startling frightened spiders from their silk,
And set the brindled muley cow to sulking,
    Refusing to give down her morning milk.

Sometimes at noon they make the cups and saucers
    In the corner cupboard shake and rattle,
The glass knobs wobble slyly on the dresser
    And the prim lid dance a jig upon the kettle.

Sometimes at night they tap against the bolster,
    And the little curly bedsprings wake and squeak,
And all the chintz and scrim begin to whisper,
    And the joints of the four-poster softly creak.

The rapping spirits visit Mrs. Wevvle
    Any time of any night or day.
Are they from the Lord or from the Devil?
    If Mrs. Wevvle knows, she doesn't say.

THIS IS MY HOUSE

This little white house belongs to me;
    Rain, you may not come in.
Sun, stroke not the paint so possessively,
    You are likely to wear it thin.

Wind, why do you howl and pommel my door
    Morning and evening long?
The hinges, which never have yielded before,
    Are still defiant and strong.

Oh, my little white house will be yours some day
    When the days of my years are all done;
Be kind to it then, O wind, I pray;
    Be gentle, O rain and sun.

BIG BLACK DOG

Big black dog, is life so dull
That you seek your pleasure chasing my bull?

Big black dog, stop running my cows;
Get away fast to your master's house;

It's there you belong in your own back lot
Where somebody loves you; I do not.

You have no right on my pasture paths
Terrorizing my little calves.

I know a man with a ready gun
Who wants a good target; you might be one.

Big black dog, better listen to me:
A big black bird sits waiting in a tree,

Old turkey buzzard on a walnut limb,
And I don't like the looks of him.

His eyes are sharp and hungry too,
And I think they're staring down at you.

ANGUS IN A HEREFORD PASTURE

The Herefords stared at first: his blackness was so black,
Not even a Hereford-style white line to grace his back,
This new one. Not as though they wished him gone away,
Not as though they hoped that he would stay.
Theirs was just a cool and contemplative gaze
Asserting their nature-given privilege to appraise
Such sudden stranger come, such sleek dark thing.
He returned their stare in kind. If he was pondering
How faces could be stamped so winter-snowy white
On hides so red while his was black as starless night,
He did not voice such wonder. He bent his shapely head,
As all his pastureland companions likewise did,
And began to graze the lush green hill, none caring whether
A breed was black or red — they were bovines all, together,
One herd, content with grass and rain-washed autumn weather.

LITTLE OLD LADY IN A BIG OLD HOUSE

Windows too high to reach for easy cleaning,
    Too much stooping, scouring long, wide floors,
Belongings losing much of useful meaning,
    Too many seldom closed and opened doors.

Too many rooms she has no longer need of,
    Over-spaciousness of lawn to mow,
Repairs potential that she must take heed of,
    Too many tasks for hands becoming slow.

Reason tells her when there's time to listen
    Of small new dwellings easier to keep;
Reason asks her why she clings to this one;
    She ponders that before she goes to sleep

Sometimes. But when she thinks to pamper
    Her life with more of ease and move away,
Her Lares and Penates start to whimper –
    They always do – and she decides to stay.

INFLECTION

The hoot owl questions,
    The mockingbird quotes,
The tree frog is given
    To tentative notes.

But the katydid's voice
    In bush or tree
Is the positive voice
    Of authority.

Whatever it is
    That the katydid states,
She avers, she avows,
    She asseverates.

TWILIGHT CALL

    Come, sheep,
Bring your lambs and come to the fold;
The night has dangers the day doesn't hold,
Dangers that slither and crawl and creep,
Dangers that crouch and dangers that leap.

    Come, sheep,
Sunlight is warm, but the sun has set;
Starlight is cold and grass is wet.
The lambs will shiver against the hill,
Sky cannot shelter; roof shingles will.

    Come, sheep,
The walls of the shed are strong and tight
Against the wind, against the night;
Straw lies clean and deep on the floor,
And the shepherd calls at the sheepcote door,
    Come, sheep, sheep, sheep, sheep.

PENNIES

To Mr. McGivry it's nothing strange,
Buying or selling, to arrange
For tarnished pennies with his change.

He takes them home and scrubs them clean
And rubs them to a lustrous sheen.
He leaves no smudges to demean

Indian head or Lincoln face:
A blemish is "a wee disgrace"
On the honored coinage of a race.

He hands them out to those he greets,
Friends and strangers whom he meets,
Or children playing in the streets.

When anybody asks him why,
Ever terse and ever shy,
He always makes the same reply

In the mild McGivry way,
"Puts bright spots on a person's day."
And that is all he cares to say.

I hope when Mr. McGivry dies,
Someone will kindly close his eyes
With burnished coppers where he lies,

Coins that gleam with golden light.
Mr. McGivry has a right
To bright spots shining on his night.

SPRING SONG IN JANUARY

A glowering sky is dripping snow
    And frozen rain and balls of sleet;
People walk their ice-paved ways
    On cautious, tense, unstable feet.

Icicle tridents hang from the eaves,
    Sharp-whittled by the flinty cold,
And pierce the darkling atmosphere
    As Neptune pronged gray seas of old.

Mottled, snow-splotched evergreens,
    Cedars, cypresses and pines,
Shudder when the north wind howls,
    Shiver when the west wind whines.

But somewhere South the mockingbird,
    Not very near, not very far,
Already tunes his vibrant throat
    And rehearses his Northland repertoire.

Bessie Marlin Mason is a native Hoosier. A graduate of Indiana University, she was elected to Phi Beta Kappa. She was an English teacher at Purdue University until she retired several years ago. Her publishing credits include numerous appearances in Saturday Evening Post, Good Housekeeping, Sparrow, *and many other journals and reviews, both large and small. She was represented in the popular Sparrow Press-Purdue Poets Cooperative anthology* Indiana Indiana *published in 1976. The poems in this book celebrate her home, Cedar Hill, near Bloomington, Indiana, and authentically reflect a tradition still flourishing.*

Back issues of Sparrow available on microfilm

Arrangements have been made with University Microfilms of the Xerox Corporation to provide a full run of back issues of Sparrow. Please order from University Microfilms Services, 301 North Zeeb Road, Ann Arbor, Michigan 48016.